Big Balloon

by Jay Dale
photography by Ned Meldrum

It is fun to play with a balloon.

You can get:

a balloon

a bottle

a funnel

yeast

warm water

sugar

a spoon

3

My red balloon
can go up like this.

My red balloon
can go down like this.

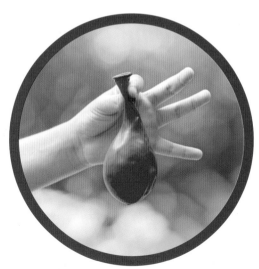

The sugar goes in the water.

The yeast goes in the water, too.

The spoon goes in the water like this.

The funnel goes inside the bottle.

Look!
The water and sugar
and yeast
go into the bottle.

9

The balloon goes on the bottle.

The balloon and the bottle
can sit on the table in the sun.

Look at the balloon.
It is bigger.

Look at the balloon.
It is bigger and bigger!

You can play with a balloon, too!
Will your balloon get
bigger and **bigger?**

Balloons are fun to play with.
You can play with a balloon, too!